First Facts®

The Solar System

Revised and Updated

Uranus

by Thomas K. Adamson

Consultant:
Stephen J. Kortenkamp, PhD
Research Scientist
Planetary Science Institute, Tucson, Arizona

Capstone press®

Mankato, Minnesota

First Facts is published by Capstone Press,
151 Good Counsel Drive, P.O. Box 669, Mankato, Minnesota 56002.
www.capstonepress.com

Library of Congress Cataloging-in-Publication Data
Adamson, Thomas K., 1970–
    Uranus / by Thomas K. Adamson.—Rev. and updated.
    p. cm.—(First facts. The Solar system)
    Includes bibliographical references and index.
    ISBN-13: 978-1-4296-0730-8 (hardcover : alk. paper)
    ISBN-10: 1-4296-0730-0 (hardcover : alk. paper)
    1. Uranus (Planet)—Juvenile literature. I. Title. II. Series.
QB681.A33 2008
523.47—dc22   2007003538

Summary: Discusses the orbit, atmosphere, surface features, and exploration of the
    planet Uranus.

Editorial Credits
Gillia Olson, editor; Juliette Peters, designer and illustrator; Jo Miller, photo researcher;
    Scott Thoms, photo editor

Photo Credits
Astronomical Society of the Pacific/NASA, 5, 14
Corbis/Bettmann, 20
NASA/JPL, cover, 1, 4
Photodisc planet images within illustrations and chart, 6–7, 11, 13, 19, 21
Photo Researchers Inc./Science Photo Library/Mark Garlick, 15
Space Images/NASA/JPL, 8, 9; NASA & Kenneth Seidelmann/U.S. Naval Observatory, 16

Table of Contents

Voyager 2 and Uranus

When *Voyager 2* flew by Uranus in 1986, scientists were surprised. The **spacecraft's** pictures showed a plain blue ball. Scientists thought the planet would look more exciting. Since then, powerful telescopes have taken more pictures. Uranus is not as plain as it looks.

Fast Facts about Uranus

Diameter: 31,764 miles (51,118 kilometers)
Average Distance from Sun: 1.78 billion miles (2.87 billion kilometers)
Average Temperature (cloud top): minus 315 degrees Fahrenheit (minus 193 degrees Celsius)
Length of Day: 17 hours, 14 minutes
Length of Year: 84 Earth years
Moons: at least 27
Rings: 11

5

The Solar System

Uranus is the seventh planet from the Sun. It is one of the gas giants, along with Jupiter, Saturn, and Neptune. The rocky planets closest to the Sun are Mercury, Venus, Earth, and Mars.

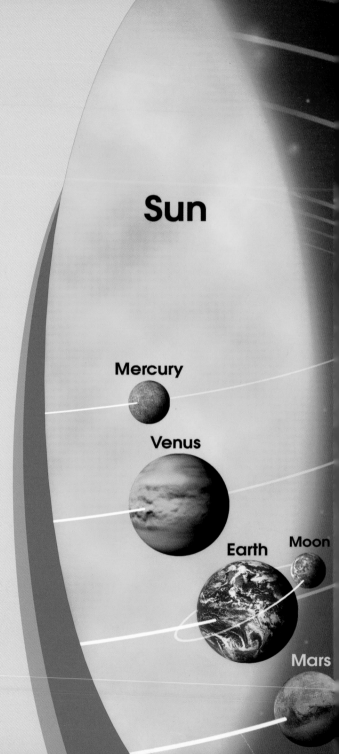

Sun

Mercury

Venus

Earth

Moon

Mars

Jupiter

Saturn

Uranus

Neptune

7

Uranus' Atmosphere

The gases surrounding a planet are called its **atmosphere**. Uranus has methane gas in its atmosphere. Methane causes the planet's pale blue color.

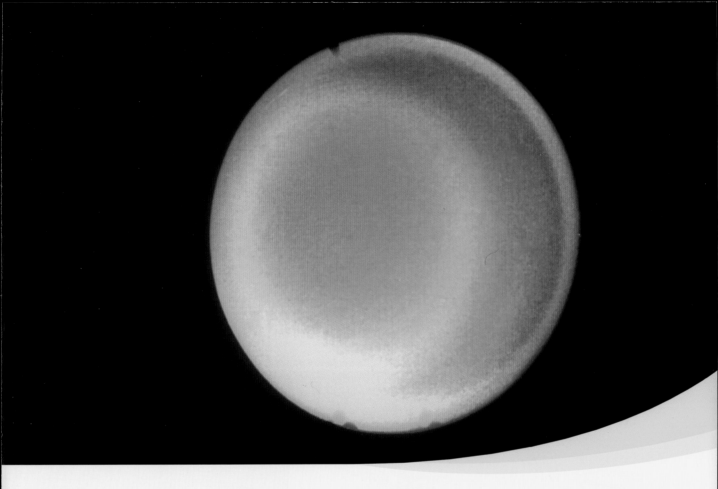

Uranus has faint, fast-moving clouds.
Scientists color pictures of the clouds
using computers. The clouds are then
easier to see.

Uranus' Makeup

Uranus does not have a solid surface under its atmosphere like Earth does. Instead, most of the planet is a soupy layer of ice and gases. Uranus does have a **core** of ice and rock.

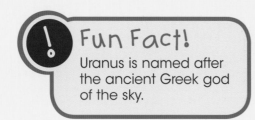

Fun Fact!
Uranus is named after the ancient Greek god of the sky.

How Uranus Moves

Like all the planets, Uranus spins as it circles the Sun. Uranus spins on its **axis** once every 17 hours, 14 minutes. It circles the Sun once every 84 years.

Uranus is also different from other planets. It spins on its side. Something probably smashed into Uranus to make it spin sideways.

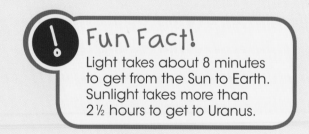

! Fun Fact!

Light takes about 8 minutes to get from the Sun to Earth. Sunlight takes more than 2½ hours to get to Uranus.

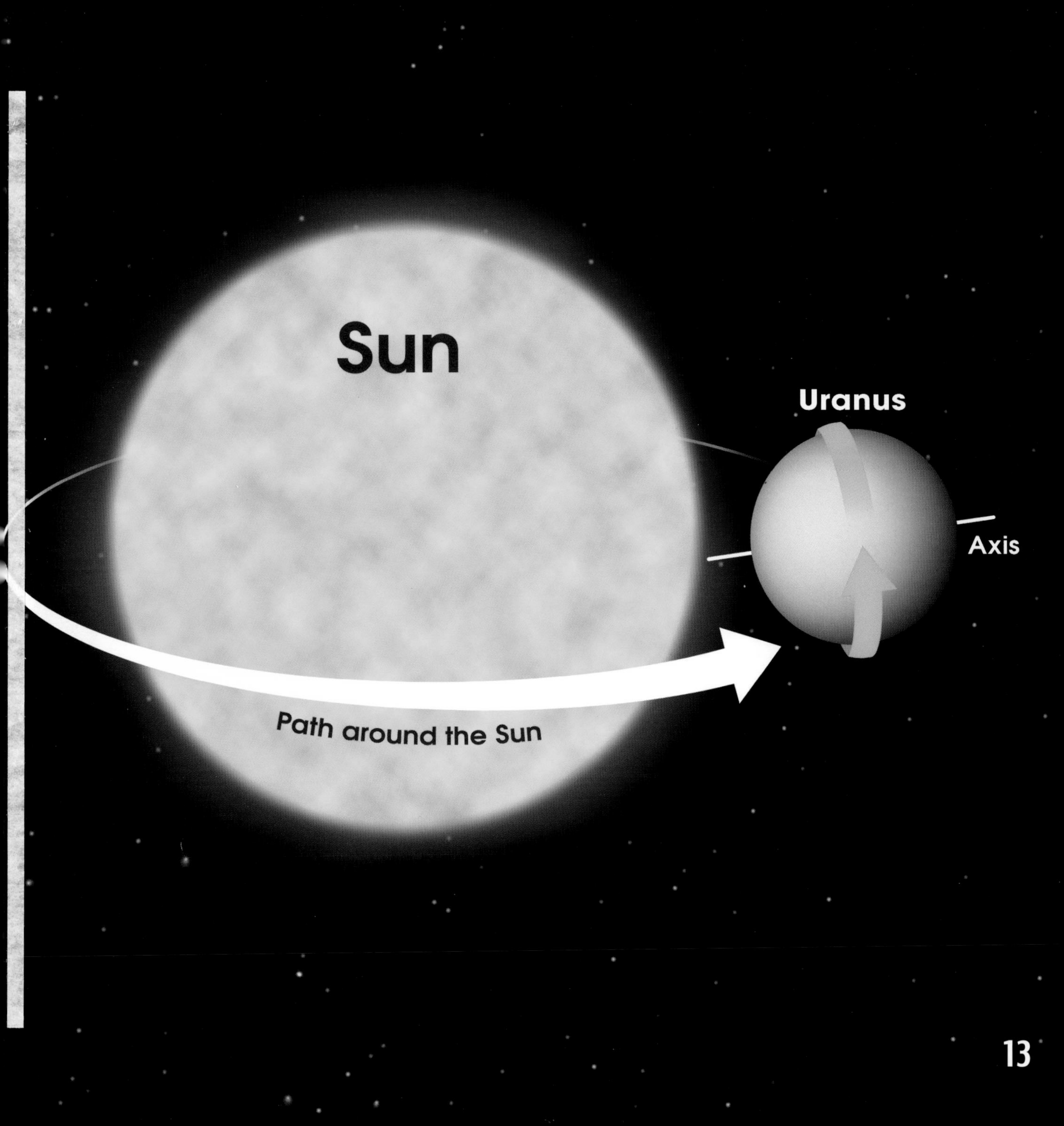

Sun

Uranus

Axis

Path around the Sun

Miranda

Moons and Rings

Uranus has at least 27 moons.
Miranda has giant **canyons** and deep
grooves. Umbriel has a strange mark
that looks like a doughnut.

Eleven rings circle Uranus. They are made of dust and chunks of ice. The rings are very dark and hard to see. Artists' paintings show how they circle the planet.

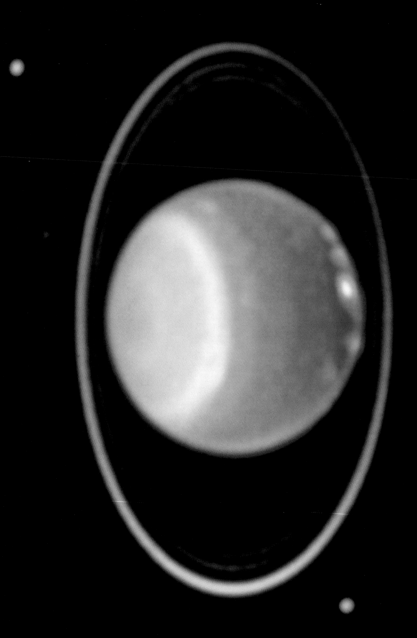

Studying Uranus

Only one spacecraft has flown by Uranus. No new missions are planned. Today, scientists study Uranus with **telescopes**. Pictures from the Hubble Space Telescope show more clouds on Uranus than ever seen before.

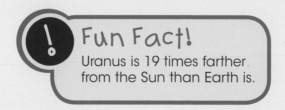

Fun Fact!
Uranus is 19 times farther from the Sun than Earth is.

Comparing Uranus to Earth

Uranus and Earth are very different. Earth is a rocky, solid planet. Uranus is mostly gas and ice. People could not breathe in Uranus' atmosphere. People could not live there.

Fun Fact!
Uranus is four times as wide as Earth.

Size Comparison

Uranus

Earth

Amazing but True!

Uranus was the first planet discovered with a telescope. The planets closer to the Sun were all discovered without telescopes. Without a telescope, Uranus is very hard to see. William Herschel, with the help of his sister Caroline, discovered the planet in 1781. They used a telescope that William had built.

Planet Comparison Chart

Planet	Size Rank (1=largest)	Makeup	1 Trip around the Sun (Earth Time)
Mercury	8	rock	88 days
Venus	6	rock	225 days
Earth	5	rock	365 days, 6 hours
Mars	7	rock	687 days
Jupiter	1	gases and ice	11 years, 11 months
Saturn	2	gases and ice	29 years, 6 months
Uranus	3	gases and ice	84 years
Neptune	4	gases and ice	164 years, 10 months

Glossary

atmosphere (AT-muhss-feehr)—the layer of gases that surrounds some planets and moons

axis (AK-siss)—an imaginary line that runs through the middle of a planet or moon; a planet spins on its axis.

canyon (KAN-yuhn)—a long, deep valley with steep sides

core (KOR)—the inner part of a planet that usually is made of metal or rock

spacecraft (SPAYSS-kraft)—a vehicle that travels in space

telescope (TEL-uh-skope)—an instrument that makes distant objects seem larger and closer

Read More

Olien, Rebecca. *Exploring the Planets in Our Solar System.* Objects in the Sky. New York: PowerKids Press, 2007.

Orme, Helen, and David Orme. *Let's Explore Uranus.* Milwaukee: Gareth Stevens, 2007.

Taylor-Butler, Christine. *Uranus.* Scholastic News Nonfiction Readers. New York: Children's Press, 2007.

Internet Sites

FactHound offers a safe, fun way to find Internet sites related to this book. All of the sites on FactHound have been researched by our staff.

Here's how:
1. Visit *www.facthound.com*
2. Choose your grade level.
3. Type in this book ID **1429607300** for age-appropriate sites. You may also browse subjects by clicking on letters, or by clicking on pictures and words.
4. Click on the **Fetch It** button.

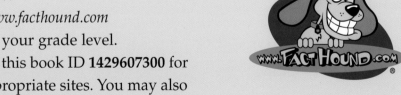

FactHound will fetch the best sites for you!

Index